# Angling
## to
# Zorbing

Sports from A to Z

Mary Elizabeth Salzmann

Consulting Editor, Diane Craig, M.A./Reading Specialist

Published by ABDO Publishing Company, 8000 West 78th Street, Edina, Minnesota 55439. Copyright © 2008 by Abdo Consulting Group, Inc. International copyrights reserved in all countries. No part of this book may be reproduced in any form without written permission from the publisher. Super SandCastle™ is a trademark and logo of ABDO Publishing Company.

Printed in the United States.

Editor: Pam Price
Consulting Editor: Diane Craig, M.A./Reading Specialist
Content Developer: Nancy Tuminelly
Cover and Interior Design and Production: Mighty Media
Photo Credits: BananaStock Ltd., Comstock, Corel, Digital Vision, iStockphoto (Brian McEntire, Lawrence Sawyer, unknown), JupiterImages Corporation, Photodisc, Rubberball Productions, Liz Salzmann, ShutterStock, Karen Spruth, Tim de Waele/Corbis, Zorb Ltd./www.zorb.com

Library of Congress Cataloging-in-Publication Data

Salzmann, Mary Elizabeth, 1968-

  Angling to zorbing : sports from A to Z / Mary Elizabeth Salzmann.

    p. cm. --  (Let's see A to Z)

  ISBN 978-1-59928-881-9

  1.  Sports--Juvenile literature. 2.  English language--Alphabet--Juvenile literature.  I. Title.

  GV705.4.S35 2008

  796--dc22

                        2007015626

Super SandCastle™ books are created by a team of professional educators, reading specialists, and content developers around five essential components—phonemic awareness, phonics, vocabulary, text comprehension, and fluency—to assist young readers as they develop reading skills and strategies and increase their general knowledge. All books are written, reviewed, and leveled for guided reading, early reading intervention, and Accelerated Reader® programs for use in shared, guided, and independent reading and writing activities to support a balanced approach to literacy instruction.

# About Super Sandcastle™

## Bigger Books for Emerging Readers
## Grades PreK–3

Created for library, classroom, and at-home use, Super SandCastle™ books support and engage young readers as they develop and build literacy skills and will increase their general knowledge about the world around them. Super SandCastle™ books are part of SandCastle™, the leading PreK–3 imprint for emerging and beginning readers. Super SandCastle™ features a larger trim size for more reading fun.

## Let Us Know

Super SandCastle™ would like to hear your stories about reading this book. What was your favorite page? Was there something hard that you needed help with? Share the ups and downs of learning to read. We want to hear from you! Send us an e-mail.

**sandcastle@abdopublishing.com**

Contact us for a complete list of SandCastle™, Super SandCastle™, and other nonfiction and fiction titles from ABDO Publishing Company.

www.abdopublishing.com • 8000 West 78th Street Edina, MN 55439 • 800-800-1312 • 952-831-1632 fax

This fun and informative series employs illustrated definitions to introduce emerging readers to an alphabet of words in various topic areas. Each page combines words with corresponding images and descriptive sentences to encourage learning and knowledge retention. AlphagalorZ inspires young readers to find out more about the subjects that most interest them!

The "Guess What?" feature expands the reading and learning experience by offering additional information and fascinating facts about specific words or concepts. The "More Words" section provides additional related A to Z vocabulary words that develop and increase reading comprehension.

These books are appropriate for library, classroom, and home use.

# A a

# Angling

*Angling* is another word for *fishing*.

Fishing with a net is not angling.

When you angle, you catch fish with a hook, which is usually attached to a line and a pole.

A long time ago, fishhooks were called angles.

# Baseball

In baseball, you hit the ball with a bat.

You catch the baseball with a mitt.

# Basketball

In basketball, you throw the ball through a hoop.

b

B

# Cycling

There are many kinds of cycling, including road cycling, BMX, and mountain biking.

Extreme cyclists can do tricks on their bikes.

BMX bicycle

road bicycle

mountain bicycle

# Diving

You can **dive** off of a springboard or a **diving** platform into a swimming pool.

**Divers** do flips, twists, and somersaults in the air before they hit the water.

Guess what ?

Springboards are either 1 or 3 meters high.
Diving platforms can be 5, 7.5, or 10 meters high.

7

# Equestrian

An equestrian rides horses. Equestrian sports are horse-riding competitions.

Two categories of equestrian competitions are jumping and dressage.

In dressage, the rider has the horse perform a series of steps and movements.

**Guess what** ?

*Dressage* is pronounced druh-*sahzh*.

# Figure Skating

Figure skaters do leaps and spins on the ice.

**f**

# Football

The quarterback throws the football.

A receiver catches the football.

F

# G

## Gymnastics

There are many different events in gymnastics.

### g

Some events include balance beam, floor exercise, and pommel horse.

## Golf

In golf, you use clubs to knock a little ball into a hole.

A short golf shot is called a putt.

**Guess what ?** Most golf balls have between 300 and 500 dimples.

# Handball

There are two kinds of handball.

In court handball, players take turns hitting a small ball against a wall with their hands.

In team handball, each team tries to throw a larger ball into the other team's goal.

# Ice Hockey

Ice hockey players wear ice skates, helmets, and pads.

Each team uses hockey sticks to hit the puck into the other team's goal.

# Judo

Judo is one of the martial arts.

In judo, one person tries to throw the other person to the floor and hold him or her down.

There is no punching or kicking in judo.

*Judo* means "the gentle way" in Japanese.

# Kayaking

You can kayak on a river, lake, or ocean.

A kayak paddle has a blade on each end.

**K**

**k**

# Karate

Karate is one of the martial arts.

In karate, you use kicks, punches, and blocks.

# Lacrosse

In lacrosse, players throw and catch a ball using sticks that have nets on the ends.

Each team tries to throw the ball into the other team's goal.

Lacrosse was developed from a traditional sport played by Native Americans.

# Marathon

A marathon is a running race that is 26.2 miles long.

Some marathons are huge events with thousands of runners.

m

M

# Nordic Skiing

Cross-country, jumping, and biathlon are the three **Nordic skiing** sports.

ski jumping

**N** **n**

cross-country skiing

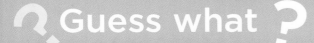
Biathlon is a combination of cross-counry skiing and rifle shooting.

# Olympic Games

In the Olympic Games, athletes from different countries compete against each other in many sports.

Winter games include ice hockey and skiing.

Summer games include boxing and softball.

The Olympic Games are held every two years, alternating between summer sports and winter sports.

# Polo

Polo players ride horses.

They use long mallets to try to hit a ball into the other team's goal.

Polo is played with either three or four players on each team.

# Q

# Quoits

**Quoits** are rings made out of rubber, metal, or rope.

The players throw the **quoits**, trying to get them to land around a post.

The post can be attached to a board or stuck in the ground.

# Rowing

Rowing boats are called shells. Shells are long and narrow and made for one to eight rowers.

# Racquetball

Racquetball players take turns hitting a small rubber ball against a wall with a racket.

r

R

In some shells, each rower pulls one oar. In other shells, each rower pulls two oars.

# Soccer

The goalkeepers are the only soccer players allowed to touch the ball with their hands.

# Swimming

The different ways of swimming are called strokes.

Swimming strokes include breaststroke, freestyle, backstroke, and butterfly.

# Tennis

T

t

Tennis players use rackets to hit a ball back and forth over a low net.

Tennis can be played by two or four players at a time.

# Ultimate

Ultimate players throw a disc to each other on a field.

A team scores when one of its players catches the disc in the other team's end zone.

**u**

**U**

**Guess what ?**

Ultimate was invented by high school students in New Jersey.

# Volleyball

Volleyball players use their arms and hands to hit a ball over a high net.

The players are not allowed to catch or throw the volleyball.

**V**

**V**

# W

# Wrestling

Wrestlers use special grips and holds to try to pin each other on the floor.

Hitting, kicking, and punching are not allowed in wrestling.

# X Games

The X Games are held every year in the summer and winter.

**X**

**X**

Summer X Games events include motocross, BMX cycling, and skateboarding.

Winter X Games events include skiing, snowmobiling, and snowboarding.

# Y y

## Yoga

Yoga is a type of exercise.

You hold your body in different positions and concentrate on breathing slowly and deeply.

## Yachting

A yacht can be a sailboat or a motorboat.

But yachting most often means racing or traveling in a sailboat.

? Guess what ?

In many cultures, yoga is a form of meditation.

# Zorbing

A Zorb is a clear plastic ball large enough for a person to fit inside.

Zorbing is getting inside a Zorb and rolling across a lawn or down a hill.

# Glossary

**alternate** – to change back and forth from one to the other.

**athlete** – someone who is good at sports or games that require strength, speed, or agility.

**category** – a group of things that have something in common.

**compete** – to try hard to outdo others in achieving a goal.

**competition** – a contest.

**concentrate** – to focus your thoughts and attention on something.

**court** – an area where sports such as basketball, tennis, and volleyball are played.

**event** – one of the activies that is part of a sports competition.

**fishhook** – a curved piece of metal with a sharp point on the end that is used for catching fish.

**goal** – points scored for getting an object into a specific area during a game.

**goalkeeper** – the player who guards the goal to keep the other team from scoring.

**grip** – a tight hold.

include – to take in as part of a group.

knock – to hit something with force.

leap – to jump or spring up from something.

mallet – a club with a long handle.

martial art – one of the styles of fighting that come from Asia.

metal – a hard, shiny substance such as iron or copper that is dug out of the earth.

net – a fabric made from strings that are knotted or woven together with holes in between. Net is used to make things such as bags, fishnets, court dividers, and goals.

perform – to do a specific action or act in a particular way.

plastic – a man-made material that is light and strong and can be made into different shapes.

platform – a raised flat surface.

punch – to hit with a closed fist.

racket – a paddle-shaped frame with a handle and crisscrossing strings that is used to hit a ball.

series – a group of related things that go in a certain order.

somersault – to turn head over heels on the ground or in the air, either forward or backward.

zone – an area that is set off for a specific use or purpose.

# More Sports Talk!

## Can you learn about these sports too?

| | | |
|---|---|---|
| aerobics | hammer throw | sailing |
| aikido | high jump | shot put |
| archery | hiking | skateboarding |
| badminton | horseshoes | snowshoeing |
| bobsledding | ice dancing | softball |
| bowling | inline skating | speed skating |
| boxing | javelin | squash |
| broomball | jujitsu | sumo |
| canoeing | kickball | surfing |
| climbing | lawn bowling | table tennis |
| cricket | long jump | tae kwon do |
| croquet | luge | track-and-field |
| curling | mountaineering | trapshooting |
| darts | orienteering | triathlon |
| decathlon | paintball | water polo |
| disc golf | pole vault | waterskiing |
| discus | relay | weight lifting |
| fencing | Roller Derby | Wiffle ball |
| field hockey | rugby | windsurfing |